for Lent 2016

SACRED
SPACE

for Lent 2016

SACRED
SPACE

from the website www.sacredspace.ie

Prayer from the Irish Jesuits

LOYOLA PRESS.
A JESUIT MINISTRY

Chicago

LOYOLA PRESS.
A JESUIT MINISTRY

3441 N. Ashland Avenue
Chicago, Illinois 60657
(800) 621-1008
www.loyolapress.com

Scripture quotations are from the *New Revised Standard Version Bible: Catholic Edition*, copyright © 1989, 1993 National Council of the Churches of Christ in the United States of America. Used by permission. All rights reserved.

Cover art credit: © iStock/Qweek

ISBN-13: 978-0-8294-4370-7
ISBN-10: 0-8294-4370-3
Library of Congress Control Number: 2015946930

15 16 17 18 19 20 Versa 10 9 8 7 6 5 4 3 2 1

Contents

The Presence of God

Bless all who worship you, almighty God,
from the rising of the sun to it setting:
from your goodness enrich us,
by your love inspire us,
by your Spirit guide us,
by your power protect us,
in your mercy receive us,
now and always.

How to Use This Booklet

During each week of Lent, begin by reading the "Something to think and pray about each day this week." Then proceed through "The Presence of God," "Freedom," and "Consciousness" steps to prepare yourself to hear the Word of God in your heart. In the next step, "The Word," turn to the Scripture reading for each day of the week. Inspiration points are provided if you need them. Then return to the "Conversation" and "Conclusion" steps. Follow this process every day of Lent.

February 10—February 13

Something to think and pray about each day this week:

Christ's "Disturbing Freshness"

If we are to nourish faith for tomorrow, we are challenged today to imagine a different quality of Christian commitment than existed before. Sixty years ago Henri de Lubac described Christ as "the great disturber" but also as the new image of God and of humanity, who brings refreshing novelty into a tired world. He was asking how we had arrived at a situation where Christianity was seen either as the enemy of full humanity, or, worse still, as a boring and empty legend. These same accusations are alive today, though in a different cultural context.

Our lived culture is nine-tenths invisible: it contains meanings and values that underlie a whole way of life. We live by unstated and unexamined perceptions. But this world of images and values has immense, if often unconscious, impact on our capacity for life decisions, including, of course, the decision about faith in God.

It is a liberation to realize, with Cardinal John Henry Newman, that existential truth can only be found when the whole person is involved: some forms of knowledge are accessible only through love. Many are now seeking a spiritual consciousness beyond the confusion and fragmentation of our day. There is a hunger, less shy or silent than it was a generation back, for something more, which Christians may identify as the "disturbing freshness of Christ."

The Presence of God

Be still and know that I am God. Lord, may your spirit guide me to seek your loving presence more and more. For it is there I find rest and refreshment from this busy world.

Freedom

Everything has the potential to draw forth from me a fuller love and life. Yet my desires are often fixed, caught on illusions of fulfillment. I ask that God through my freedom may orchestrate my desires in a vibrant, loving melody rich in harmony.

Consciousness

At this moment, Lord, I turn my thoughts to you. I will set aside my chores and preoccupations. I will take rest and refreshment in your presence, Lord.

The Word

I read the Word of God slowly, a few times over, and I listen to what God is saying to me. (Please turn to the Scripture on the following pages. Inspiration points are provided should you need them. When you are ready, return here to continue.)

Conversation

Sometimes I wonder what I might say if I were to meet you in person, Lord. I think I might say, "Thank you, Lord" for always being there for me.

Conclusion

Glory be to the Father, and to the Son, and to the Holy Spirit, as it was in the beginning, is now and ever shall be, world without end. Amen.

Wednesday 10th February
Ash Wednesday
Matthew 6:1–6, 16–18

"Beware of practicing your piety before others in order to be seen by them; for then you have no reward from your Father in heaven. So whenever you give alms, do not sound a trumpet before you, as the hypocrites do in the synagogues and in the streets, so that they may be praised by others. Truly I tell you, they have received their reward. But when you give alms, do not let your left hand know what your right hand is doing, so that your alms may be done in secret; and your Father who sees in secret will reward you. And whenever you pray, do not be like the hypocrites; for they love to stand and pray in the synagogues and at the street corners, so that they may be seen by others. Truly I tell you, they have received their reward. But whenever you pray, go into your room and shut the door and pray to your Father who is in secret; and your Father who sees in secret will reward you. And whenever you fast, do not look dismal, like the hypocrites, for they disfigure their faces so as to show others that they are fasting. Truly I tell you, they have received their reward. But when you fast, put oil on your head and wash your face, so that your fasting may be seen not by others but by your Father who is in secret; and your Father who sees in secret will reward you."

- Today, Ash Wednesday, Christians all over the world begin the penitential but joyous season of Lent. Whatever we do in Lent should bring us ever closer to Jesus and prepare us to celebrate his resurrection at Easter.

- The beginning of Lent is good news: God is near and nothing can keep us from God. Jesus will find that himself later on. Anything we do in Lent is intended to bring us to God and believe the good news. Fasting, prayers, and almsgiving are ways to God, not to misery. But they can be motivated by selfishness or generosity. Key to our choices is where our hearts are. Is my heart set on God alone? Do I sometimes set out to get praise and admiration?

Thursday 11th February
Luke 9:22–25

Jesus said to his disciples: "The Son of Man must undergo great suffering, and be rejected by the elders, chief priests, and scribes, and be killed, and on the third day be raised." Then he said to them all, "If any want to become my followers, let them deny themselves and take up their cross daily and follow me. For those who want to save their life will lose it, and those who lose their life for my sake will save it. What does it profit them if they gain the whole world, but lose or forfeit themselves?"

- Jesus states clearly that his project to save the world will end in earthly disaster for himself. I sit with him in silence and gratitude that he does not simply give up and abandon humankind to its malice.

- Let me also chat with him about the things I endure. He is not saying that suffering is good, but that I can either accept it patiently or try to reject it. He looks hard at me and says, "You could spend your life just looking after yourself and trying to avoid pain and hurt. Or you can embrace the world with love and risk failure, betrayal, and disappointment from those you try to serve. Of course you will get hurt, but an eternal blessing will be yours at the End." I respond: "Lord, let me live my life as you lived yours." He thanks me.

Friday 12th February
Matthew 9:14–15

The disciples of John came to Jesus, saying, "Why do we and the Pharisees fast often, but your disciples do not fast?" And Jesus said to them, "The wedding guests cannot mourn as long as the bridegroom is with them, can they? The days will come when the bridegroom is taken away from them, and then they will fast."

- We can often feel like John's disciples, confused and unsure about what to do. The divisions in the church upset us. But Jesus is saying, "With my coming, a wedding has started; a new creation is under way. Be joyful!"

- John's disciples are waiting in the wrong place. I must stop living in no-man's land. I must wake up—the savior of the world has come, and I must join him.

Saturday 13th February
Luke 5:27–32

Jesus went out and saw a tax collector named Levi, sitting at the tax booth; and he said to him, "Follow me." And he got up, left everything, and followed him. Then Levi gave a great banquet for him in his house; and there was a large crowd of tax collectors and others sitting at the table with them. The Pharisees and their scribes were complaining to his disciples, saying, "Why do you eat and drink with tax collectors and sinners?" Jesus answered, "Those who are well have no need of a physician, but those who are sick; I have come to call not the righteous but sinners to repentance."

- Tax collectors were despised; they were social and religious outcasts. Why then does Jesus choose Levi out of all possible candidates? Because he is determined to break down dramatically the barriers that fragment human community.

- The banquet points to "table fellowship": eating and drinking together shows that the guests accept one another. Because Jesus is the main guest, we are shown that if we want to be with him at the table, we must accept the companionship of people we previously despised. At the Eucharist Jesus invites everyone to participate, not simply as individuals but as fellow disciples who are both sinners and forgiven. Do I "complain" about this?

The First Week of Lent
February 14—February 20

Something to think and pray about each day this week:

The Joyful Season

The season of Lent has begun. Lent originally meant "springtime," and so we can view it as a springtime for the spirit. It is a time also to spring clean the cave of our hearts!

Whatever the variations in the practice of Lent over the last 2,000 years, the main issue is whether Lent helps me to become more aware of how I stand in relation to God and my neighbor. The ancient practices designed to achieve these goals were fasting, almsgiving, and prayer. The call to fast makes me focus on the affairs of the spirit rather than of the body. The call to almsgiving makes me more alert to my needy neighbor. The call to prayer nourishes my relationship with God, and especially with Jesus in his Passion. What about fasting? There are many little things I can perhaps do without. The point is that the shock to the system should lead to a deeper sense of what God may want of me!

Jesus warns us against trying to attract notice when we fast or pray or give alms (Matthew 6). The simple act of washing off the ashes on Ash Wednesday is understood in some Christian circles as a reminder of Jesus' admonition to look joyous! Lent is a "joyful season."

The Presence of God

At any time of the day or night we can call on Jesus. He is always waiting, listening for our call. What a wonderful blessing. No phone needed, no e-mails, just a whisper.

Freedom

If God were trying to tell me something, would I know? If God were reassuring me or challenging me, would I notice? I ask for the grace to be free of my own preoccupations and open to what God may be saying to me.

Consciousness

How do I find myself today? Where am I with God? With others? Do I have something to be grateful for? Then I give thanks. Is there something I am sorry for? Then I ask forgiveness.

The Word

God speaks to each one of us individually. I listen attentively to hear what he is saying to me. Read the text a few times, then listen. (Please turn to the Scripture on the following pages. Inspiration points are provided should you need them. When you are ready, return here to continue.)

Conversation
What is stirring in me as I pray? Am I consoled, troubled, left cold? I imagine Jesus himself standing or sitting at my side, and I share my feelings with him.

Conclusion
I thank God for these few moments we have spent alone together and for any insights I may have been given concerning the text.

Sunday 14th February
First Sunday of Lent
Luke 4:1–13

Jesus, full of the Holy Spirit, returned from the Jordan and was led by the Spirit in the wilderness, where for forty days he was tempted by the devil. He ate nothing at all during those days, and when they were over, he was famished. The devil said to him, "If you are the Son of God, command this stone to become a loaf of bread." Jesus answered him, "It is written, 'One does not live by bread alone.'" Then the devil led him up and showed him in an instant all the kingdoms of the world. And the devil said to him, "To you I will give their glory and all this authority; for it has been given over to me, and I give it to anyone I please. If you, then, will worship me, it will all be yours." Jesus answered him, "It is written, 'Worship the Lord your God, and serve only him.'" Then the devil took him to Jerusalem, and placed him on the pinnacle of the temple, saying to him, "If you are the Son of God, throw yourself down from here, for it is written, 'He will command his angels concerning you, to protect you,' and 'On their hands they will bear you up, so that you will not dash your foot against a stone.'" Jesus answered him, "It is said, 'Do not put the Lord your God to the test.'" When the devil had finished every test, he departed from him until an opportune time.

- In the wilderness Jesus did not engage the devil's temptations. He simply quoted the Word of God in Scripture. God's Word has power, even over demons.

- Jesus' experience teaches us that there is nothing wrong with being tempted; it's how we react to the temptation that matters. A short prayer or a quote from God's Word will help us let it go. For example: "Lead me not into temptation" or "I must forgive, not once but seventy times."

Monday 15th February
Matthew 25:31–46

Jesus said to his disciples, "When the Son of Man comes in his glory, and all the angels with him, then he will sit on the throne of his glory. All the nations will be gathered before him, and he will separate people one from another as a shepherd separates the sheep from the goats, and he will put the sheep at his right hand and the goats at the left. Then the king will say to those at his right hand, 'Come, you that are blessed by my Father, inherit the kingdom prepared for you from the foundation of the world; for I was hungry and you gave me food, I was thirsty and you gave me something to drink, I was a stranger and you welcomed me, I was naked and you gave me clothing, I was sick and you took care of me, I was in prison and you visited me.' Then the righteous will answer him, 'Lord, when was it that we saw you hungry and gave you food, or thirsty and gave you something to drink? And when was it that we saw you a stranger and welcomed you, or naked and gave you clothing? And when was it that we saw you sick or in prison and visited you?' And the king will answer them, 'Truly I tell you, just as you did it to one of the least of these who are members of my family, you did it to me.' Then he will say to those at his left hand, 'You that are accursed, depart from me into the eternal fire prepared for the devil and his angels; for I was hungry and you gave me no food, I was thirsty and you gave me nothing to drink, I was a stranger and you did not welcome me, naked and you did not give me clothing, sick and in prison and you did not visit me.' Then they also will answer, 'Lord, when was it that we saw you hungry or thirsty or a stranger or naked or sick or in prison, and did not take care of you?' Then he will answer them, 'Truly I tell you, just as you did not do it to one of the least of these, you did not do it to me.' And these will go away into eternal punishment, but the righteous into eternal life."

- This long and exciting parable has a simple message: "Minister to the needy around you, or else you are missing the whole point of living!" Saint Matthew's hearers had difficulty with what would happen to non-Jews, since they themselves were the Chosen People. Jesus says that with his coming into the world, everyone is a "chosen person." Everyone is to be treated with limitless respect. This is the way to get ready for God's final community of love. Jesus is already present but in disguise, in every person. Only at the End will he and they be revealed "in glory."

• What do I see when I see the needy? Do I focus on the hidden glory of others? How would I fare if human history were to be terminated today?

Tuesday 16th February
Matthew 6:7–15

Jesus said, "When you are praying, do not heap up empty phrases as the Gentiles do; for they think that they will be heard because of their many words. Do not be like them, for your Father knows what you need before you ask him. Pray then in this way: Our Father in heaven, hallowed be your name. Your kingdom come. Your will be done, on earth as it is in heaven. Give us this day our daily bread. And forgive us our debts, as we also have forgiven our debtors. And do not bring us to the time of trial, but rescue us from the evil one. For if you forgive others their trespasses, your heavenly Father will also forgive you; but if you do not forgive others, neither will your Father forgive your trespasses."

- As you pray now, is God a distant figure with little interest in your affairs? And what about your day: is God around or are you alone? The good news is that God is indescribably close to us as we go about our affairs. "Your Father knows what you need before you ask him." We might say that God is infinite awareness, and that his focus is on us. "God is closer to me than I am to myself," said Saint Augustine.

- Try to imagine that God is with you every moment of this day. He is with you as someone who loves you and who knows all you need. He is always helping you, especially as you try to bring God's values into your everyday life.

Wednesday 17th February
Luke 11:29–32

When the crowds were increasing, Jesus began to say, "This generation is an evil generation; it asks for a sign, but no sign will be given to it except the sign of Jonah. For just as Jonah became a sign to the people of Nineveh, so the Son of Man will be to this generation. The queen of the South will rise at the judgment with the people of this generation and condemn them, because she came from the ends of the earth to listen to the wisdom of Solomon, and see, something greater than Solomon is here! The people of Nineveh will rise up at the judgment with this generation and condemn it, because they repented at the proclamation of Jonah, and see, something greater than Jonah is here!"

- Jesus uses imagination in trying to help his audience catch on to the mystery of who he is. So he reminds them of famous characters in stories they already know well. He then tries to open their minds further by saying twice that "something greater" is here in his person. This is a mysterious assertion. But God is mysterious, so coming closer to the truth about God means being led along the path of mystery. Do I cultivate my capacity for mystery, or do I live on the surface of life? Do I reduce the wonders of nature and the cosmos to mere facts, or do I allow myself to ponder what their author must be like?

- Everything is a divine mystery since all comes from God. Let me sit with Jesus and ask him to enliven the mystical dimension that may be dormant in me.

Thursday 18th February
Matthew 7:7–12

Jesus said, "Ask, and it will be given to you; search, and you will find; knock, and the door will be opened for you. For everyone who asks receives, and everyone who searches finds, and for everyone who knocks, the door will be opened. Is there anyone among you who, if your child asks for bread, will give a stone? Or if the child asks for a fish, will give a snake? If you then, who are evil, know how to give good gifts to your children, how much more will your Father in heaven give good things to those who ask him! In everything do to others as you would have them do to you; for this is the law and the prophets."

• Is this gospel true? So often, our prayers seem to go unheard or unanswered. But good things happen in God's own time. A woman had a son who was very troubled since childhood. He had an inner rage that showed itself in destructive behavior. Often she bore the brunt of his anger. Not surprisingly, he lurched from one disaster to the next. He lost a number of jobs and a number of partners. Currently he has few prospects. But now in his forties, he has become reflective, and his style is changing. He is gentler, and though he is unemployed, last Christmas he scraped up some money and bought thoughtful little gifts for the

important people in his life. He and his mother
have begun to chat about things in ways that were
never possible before. Thirty-five years of prayer
are being answered.

• Jesus does not say that we will be given precisely
what we ask for; or that we will find exactly what
we are looking for; or that the particular door we
want will be opened to us. But we will receive
"good things"!

Friday 19th February
Matthew 5:20–26

Jesus said, "For I tell you, unless your righteousness
exceeds that of the scribes and the Pharisees, you will
never enter the kingdom of heaven. You have heard
that it was said to those of ancient times, 'You shall
not murder'; and 'whoever murders shall be liable to
judgment.' But I say to you that if you are angry with
a brother or sister, you will be liable to judgment; and
if you insult a brother or sister, you will be liable to
the council; and if you say, 'You fool,' you will be liable to the hell of fire. So when you are offering your
gift at the altar, if you remember that your brother
or sister has something against you, leave your gift
there before the altar and go; first be reconciled to
your brother or sister, and then come and offer your
gift. Come to terms quickly with your accuser while

you are on the way to court with him, or your accuser may hand you over to the judge, and the judge to the guard, and you will be thrown into prison. Truly I tell you, you will never get out until you have paid the last penny."

- Scribes and Pharisees were righteous and were people of the law. Jesus asks for more—for the compassion that sees beyond the law and people's weaknesses to the glory and love of God in each and all.

- The standards operating in the kingdom of heaven are high! Jesus does not dismiss Old Testament teaching, but he goes to the root of things. We can be smug and content with our conventional good behavior. Jesus, however, says to us: "But what about your anger? What about insulting someone? Do you despise anyone, ever? Such behavior won't do anymore."

Saturday 20th February
Matthew 5:43–48

Jesus said to his disciples, "You have heard that it was said, 'You shall love your neighbor and hate your enemy.' But I say to you, Love your enemies and pray for those who persecute you, so that you may be children of your Father in heaven; for he makes his sun rise on the evil and on the good, and sends rain on the righteous and on the unrighteous. For if you love those who love you, what reward do you have? Do not even the tax collectors do the same? And if you greet only your brothers and sisters, what more are you doing than others? Do not even the Gentiles do the same? Be perfect, therefore, as your heavenly Father is perfect."

- Again Jesus shows how high the standards are in the new community he is establishing. This new community is no mere human one: at the heart of it is God. So all its relationships will have a divine quality. If we want to be "children of our Father in heaven," our hearts must embrace our enemies in genuine love.

- Before Jesus came, God was portrayed as destroying the wicked. But Jesus portrays God as pouring out good things on wicked as well as good people. This seems like extravagant madness. But when we come to the Passion, we find Jesus doing what he talks about here. He pours out divine love on everyone, bad and good. He prays for his enemies. On the world scene today, we have plenty of people to love and to pray for!

The Second Week of Lent
February 21—February 27

Something to think and pray about each day this week:

God at Work in the World

A long tradition in spirituality identified union with God as being found solely in contemplative prayer. In that tradition it was understood that we can only unite ourselves with God through uniting our spirit with God, who is Spirit.

This means leaving behind this material, messy, chaotic world and climbing the mountain, as Jesus did with Peter, James, and John. There, at the top of the mountain, far distant from the cares of this world, in contemplative prayer we enter into an intimate relationship with God. Like Peter, James, and John, we wish to remain there and enjoy the intimacy of union with God.

Saint Ignatius of Loyola, however, had a more complex understanding of how some of us may find union with God. Yes, he would say, climb the mountain. But you may perhaps instead be told to go back down the mountain, to this material, messy, violent world, and to find union with God through union of your will with God's will. God, he would say, labors in our world and can be found there as fully as on the mountain. Doing what God wants is what ultimately matters either for you or for the contemplative.

If we work in the world we must, again and again, climb to the top of the mountain, to be alone with God and with ourselves, our memories and desires. There we renew our strength to continue the struggle for a more just world.

The Presence of God
God is with me, but more, God is within me. Let me dwell for a moment on God's life-giving presence in my body, in my mind, and in my heart, as I sit here, right now.

Freedom
By God's grace I was born to live in freedom. Free to enjoy the pleasures he created for me. Dear Lord, grant that I may live as you intended, with complete confidence in your loving care.

Consciousness
Where do I sense hope, encouragement, and growth areas in my life? By looking back over the last few months, I may be able to see which activities and occasions have produced rich fruit. If I do notice such areas, I will determine to give those areas both time and space in the future.

The Word
I take my time to read the Word of God slowly, a few times, allowing myself to dwell on anything that strikes me. (Please turn to the Scripture on the following pages. Inspiration points are provided should you need them. When you are ready, return here to continue.)

Conversation
What feelings are rising in me as I pray and reflect on God's Word? I imagine Jesus himself sitting or standing near me, and I open my heart to him.

Conclusion
Glory be to the Father, and to the Son, and to the Holy Spirit, as it was in the beginning, is now and ever shall be, world without end. Amen.

Sunday 21st February
Second Sunday of Lent
Luke 9:28b–36

Jesus took with him Peter and John and James, and went up on the mountain to pray. And while he was praying, the appearance of his face changed, and his clothes became dazzling white. Suddenly they saw two men, Moses and Elijah, talking to him. They appeared in glory and were speaking of his departure, which he was about to accomplish at Jerusalem. Now Peter and his companions were weighed down with sleep; but since they had stayed awake, they saw his glory and the two men who stood with him. Just as they were leaving him, Peter said to Jesus, "Master, it is good for us to be here; let us make three dwellings, one for you, one for Moses, and one for Elijah"—not knowing what he said. While he was saying this, a cloud came and overshadowed them; and they were terrified as they entered the cloud. Then from the cloud came a voice that said, "This is my Son, my Chosen; listen to him!" When the voice had spoken, Jesus was found alone. And they kept silent and in those days told no one any of the things they had seen.

- "On the mountain" the three apostles had a favored glimpse of Jesus' prayer and glory. His prayer here is a conversation with Moses and Elijah. They talked about his Passion and death. This was a down-to-earth conversation about the shape of Jesus' life. Is my prayer like that?

• The appearance of Jesus' face was "changed." Even his clothing is made radiant. We know that, if we are faithful, we shall be transfigured in Jesus' glory. As Saint Paul says: "Christ in you, your hope of glory" (Colossians 1:27).

Monday 22nd February
Matthew 16:13–19

Now when Jesus came into the district of Caesarea Philippi, he asked his disciples, "Who do people say that the Son of Man is?" And they said, "Some say John the Baptist, but others Elijah, and still others Jeremiah or one of the prophets." He said to them, "But who do you say that I am?" Simon Peter answered, "You are the Messiah, the Son of the living God." And Jesus answered him, "Blessed are you, Simon son of Jonah! For flesh and blood has not revealed this to you, but my Father in heaven. And I tell you, you are Peter, and on this rock I will build my church, and the gates of Hades will not prevail against it. I will give you the keys of the kingdom of heaven, and whatever you bind on earth will be bound in heaven, and whatever you loose on earth will be loosed in heaven."

- The traditional setting for this memorable encounter in Caesarea Philippi is a lovely riverbank under a huge rocky cliff. Jesus asks: Who do people say that I am? Impetuous Peter, always ready to speak out and take risks, confesses Jesus as the Messiah. It is an inspired confession. This uneducated fisherman, who was to prove so shaky when Jesus was arrested, is rewarded with a new name, suggested by the great solid rock above them, and also with a new role, leading the people of God. Lord, you did not leave us orphans.

- The motley band of the twelve with Peter as leader would guide the future community of Jesus. They believed that Jesus was the Son of God. Our community today is somewhat similar—the motley group who are saintly and sinful but who with firm faith believe that Jesus is the Son of God. Peter is praised today within the church for his belief and faith in Jesus as the Son of the living God. This faith would lead him into times of doubt and unfaithfulness, and eventually to martyrdom. The first call in his following of Jesus was to grow in the faith that would sustain his life. May our faith do the same.

Tuesday 23rd February
Matthew 23:1–12

Jesus said to the crowds and to his disciples, "The scribes and the Pharisees sit on Moses' seat; therefore, do whatever they teach you and follow it; but do not do as they do, for they do not practice what they teach. They tie up heavy burdens, hard to bear, and lay them on the shoulders of others; but they themselves are unwilling to lift a finger to move them. They do all their deeds to be seen by others; for they make their phylacteries broad and their fringes long. They love to have the place of honor at banquets and the best seats in the synagogues, and to be greeted with respect in the marketplaces, and to have people call them rabbi. But you are not to be called rabbi, for you have one teacher, and you are all students. And call no one your father on earth, for you have one Father—the one in heaven. Nor are you to be called instructors, for you have one instructor, the Messiah. The greatest among you will be your servant. All who exalt themselves will be humbled, and all who humble themselves will be exalted."

- In Jesus people saw a whole person. He did not bother about appearing generous, or courageous, or truthful—people quickly saw that he was these things. Lord, I have only to see the history of the church to realize how easily these words are forgotten. Ecclesiastics have exalted themselves, looked for titles, and exercised leadership by domination rather than service. I need to come back to the memory of you washing your disciples' feet. Blessed are those who clean the toilets, put out the garbage, and care for the old and incontinent. We are never as close to God as when we are serving.

- Hypocrisy means play-acting, being untrue to oneself. Jesus' harshest words are reserved for this vice. He sums it up very succinctly as, "Hey, do not practice what they preach." Do I?

Wednesday 24th February
Matthew 20:17–28

While Jesus was going up to Jerusalem, he took the twelve disciples aside by themselves, and said to them on the way, "See, we are going up to Jerusalem, and the Son of Man will be handed over to the chief priests and scribes, and they will condemn him to death; then they will hand him over to the Gentiles to be mocked and flogged and crucified; and on the third day he will be raised." Then the mother of the sons of Zebedee came to him with her sons, and kneeling before him, she asked a favor of him. And he said to her, "What do you want?" She said to him, "Declare that these two sons of mine will sit, one at your right hand and one at your left, in your kingdom." But

Jesus answered, "You do not know what you are asking. Are you able to drink the cup that I am about to drink?" They said to him, "We are able." He said to them, "You will indeed drink my cup, but to sit at my right hand and at my left, this is not mine to grant, but it is for those for whom it has been prepared by my Father." When the ten heard it, they were angry with the two brothers. But Jesus called them to him and said, "You know that the rulers of the Gentiles lord it over them, and their great ones are tyrants over them. It will not be so among you; but whoever wishes to be great among you must be your servant, and whoever wishes to be first among you must be your slave; just as the Son of Man came not to be served but to serve, and to give his life a ransom for many."

- There is a sense of doom and destiny in Jesus' words. The anticipation of personal catastrophe chills the heart. When Jesus foretells the Passion, he mentions not just the handover but the flogging and mocking. It is hard to imagine the terror that must have shadowed his heart in those last weeks.

- This walk to Jerusalem is heavy with foreboding. Jesus tries to tell the twelve of the fears that fill his soul: he will be betrayed by friends and delivered to his enemies; he will hear the death sentence read over him; he will suffer injustice, mockery, humiliation, insults; he will undergo the torture of scourging and finally face a horrific death on a gallows. That is the cup you drank, Lord. If you ask me to share it, give me the strength.

Thursday 25th February
Luke 16:19–31

Jesus said to the Pharisees, "There was a rich man who was dressed in purple and fine linen and who feasted sumptuously every day. And at his gate lay a poor man named Lazarus, covered with sores, who longed to satisfy his hunger with what fell from the rich man's table; even the dogs would come and lick his sores. The poor man died and was carried away by the angels to be with Abraham. The rich man also died and was buried. In Hades, where he was being tormented, he looked up and saw Abraham far away with Lazarus by his side. He called out, 'Father Abraham, have mercy on me, and send Lazarus to dip the tip of his finger in water and cool my tongue; for I am in agony in these flames.' But Abraham said, 'Child, remember that during your lifetime you received your good things, and Lazarus in like manner evil things; but now he is comforted here, and you are in agony. Besides all this, between you and us a great chasm has been fixed, so that those who might want to pass from here to you cannot do so, and no one can cross from there to us.' He said, 'Then, father, I beg you to send him to my father's house—for I have five brothers—that he may warn them, so that they will not also come into this place of torment.' Abraham replied, 'They have Moses and the prophets; they should listen to them.' He said, 'No, father Abraham; but if someone goes to them from the dead, they will repent.' He said to him, 'If they do not listen to Moses and the prophets, neither will they be convinced even if someone rises from the dead.'"

- This is a parable of startling contrasts, but its central message is simple: be alert to the needs under your nose. It is not concerned with patterns of good living on the part of Lazarus, nor of evil-doing on the part of the rich man. But the latter closed his eyes to the needy at his gate. And without an eye for the needy around us, our life becomes self-centered and callous. Jesus is asking his listeners to open their eyes to what is around them and to open their ears to the simple commands of the gospel: love your neighbor.

- We can move too quickly through this parable—we know it and its ending well. Stay in prayer with its beginning. Nobody should be covered in sores and hungry; nobody should be comforted only by dogs. In a world of homelessness, hunger, and loneliness, should anyone be dressed so well and feast so well? One had no choice but to fast, the other had a choice to help. Saint Ignatius wrote for each day, "Who will I help today?"

Friday 26th February
Matthew 21:33–43, 45–46

Jesus said, "Listen to another parable. There was a landowner who planted a vineyard, put a fence around it, dug a wine press in it, and built a watchtower. Then he leased it to tenants and went to another country. When the harvest time had come, he sent his slaves to the tenants to collect his produce. But the tenants seized his slaves and beat one, killed another, and stoned another. Again he sent other slaves, more than the first; and they treated them in the same way. Finally he sent his son to them, saying, 'They will respect my son.' But when the tenants saw the son, they said to themselves, 'This is the heir; come, let us kill him and get his inheritance.' So they seized him, threw him out of the vineyard, and killed him. Now when the owner of the vineyard comes, what will he do to those tenants?" They said to him, "He will put those wretches to a miserable death, and lease the vineyard to other tenants who will give him the produce at the harvest time." Jesus said to them, "Have you never read in the Scriptures: 'The stone that the builders rejected has become the cornerstone; this was the Lord's doing, and it is amazing in our eyes'? Therefore I tell you, the kingdom of God will be taken away from you and given to a people that produces the fruits of the kingdom." When the chief priests and the Pharisees heard his parables, they realized that he was speaking about them. They wanted to arrest him, but they feared the crowds, because they regarded him as a prophet.

- Lord, this parable is about those who rejected Jesus, but also about me. I am the tenant of your vineyard. For me you have planted and protected a crop, and from me you expect some harvest. The fruit is for you, not for me. I may feel annoyed when you ask, but you are right to expect something of me.

- The Pharisees feared his words, because they feared how others were reacting. They were fearful because they lacked faith that deep down they were loved. Prayer is enjoying moments of being loved, and then I am happy that Jesus is speaking about me.

Saturday 27th February
Luke 15:1–3, 11–32

Now all the tax collectors and sinners were coming near to listen to him. And the Pharisees and the scribes were grumbling and saying, "This fellow welcomes sinners and eats with them." So he told them this parable: "There was a man who had two sons. The younger of them said to his father, 'Father, give me the share of the property that will belong to me.' So he divided his property between them. A few days later the younger son gathered all he had and traveled to a distant country, and there he squandered his property in dissolute living. When he had spent everything, a severe famine took place throughout that country, and he began to be in need. So he went and hired himself out to one of the citizens of that country, who sent him to his fields to feed the pigs. He would gladly have filled himself with the pods that the pigs were eating; and no one gave him anything. But when he came to himself he said, 'How many of my father's hired hands have bread enough and to spare, but here I am dying of hunger! I will get up and go to my father, and I will say to him, "Father, I have sinned against heaven and before you; I am no longer worthy to be called your son; treat me like one of your hired hands."' So he set off and went to his father. But while he was still far off, his father saw him and was filled with compassion; he ran and put his arms around him and kissed him. Then the son said to him, 'Father, I have sinned against heaven and before you; I am no longer worthy to be called your son.' But the father said to his slaves, 'Quickly, bring out a robe—the best one—and put it on him; put a ring on his finger and sandals on his feet. And get the fatted calf and kill it, and let us eat and celebrate; for this son of mine was dead and is alive again; he was lost and is found!' And they began to celebrate. Now his elder son was in the field; and when he came and approached the house, he heard music and dancing. He called one of the slaves and asked what was going on. He replied, 'Your brother has come, and your father has killed the fatted calf, because he has got him back safe and sound.' Then he became angry and refused to go in. His father came out and began to plead with him. But he answered his father, 'Listen! For all these years I have been working like a slave for you, and I have never disobeyed your command; yet you have never given me even a young goat so that I might celebrate with my friends. But when this son of yours came back, who has devoured your property with prostitutes, you killed the fatted calf for him!' Then the father said to him, 'Son, you are always with me, and all that is mine is yours. But we had to celebrate and rejoice, because this brother of yours was dead and has come to life; he was lost and has been found.'"

- In different cultures over the centuries God has been pictured in all sorts of images and imaginations. In this parable we have Jesus' image, which is astonishing: a fond father who does not stop his wastrel son from bringing shame on himself and the family, and who not merely forgives him but embraces him, interrupts his apology, and throws a big party to express his own joy. Dear Lord, whatever happens to me, let me never forget or doubt this picture of you.

- At his lowest point the younger son "came to himself." He realized the person he had become was not his real self. This story tells us that conversion is possible; we can return to our best—our truest—selves, and when we do we will find our loving God ready to welcome us home with open arms.

February 28—March 5

Something to think and pray about each day this week:

Cleansed by tears

The famous sermon on hell in James Joyce's *A Portrait of the Artist as a Young Man* exposes a schoolboy's soul tortured by sins of lust, the boy convinced that his sins are beyond forgiveness because God is great and stern.

He has, however, a glimmer of hope: his failure has not offended Our Lady. So he prays, in the words of Cardinal John Henry Newman: "God once had meant to come on earth in heavenly glory, but we sinned; and then he could not safely visit us but with a shrouded majesty and a bedimmed radiance, for he was God. So he came himself in weakness, not in power, and he sent thee, a creature, in his stead, with a creature's comeliness and luster, suited to our state. And now thy very face and form, dear Mother, speak to us of the eternal: not like earthly beauty, dangerous to look upon, but like the morning star which is thy emblem, bright and musical, breathing purity, telling of heaven and infusing peace. O harbinger of day! O light of the pilgrim! Lead us still as thou hast led. In the dark night, across the bleak wilderness, guide us on to our Lord Jesus, guide us home."

His eyes dimmed with tears, he looks humbly up to heaven and weeps for the innocence he has lost. Later he finds a chapel and emerges from the confessional, a contrite young man of sixteen now at peace with God.

The Presence of God

God is with me, but more, God is within me, giving me existence. Let me dwell for a moment on God's life-giving presence in my body, my mind, my heart, and in the whole of my life.

Freedom

"In these days, God taught me as a schoolteacher teaches a pupil" (Saint Ignatius of Loyola). I remind myself that there are things God has to teach me yet and ask for the grace to hear them and let them change me.

Consciousness

I exist in a web of relationships—links to nature, people, God. I trace out these links, giving thanks for the life that flows through them. Some links are twisted or broken: I may feel regret, anger, disappointment. I pray for the gift of acceptance and forgiveness.

The Word
The Word of God comes down to us through the Scriptures. May the Holy Spirit enlighten my mind and my heart to respond to the gospel teachings. (Please turn to the Scripture on the following pages. Inspiration points are provided should you need them. When you are ready, return here to continue.)

Conversation
Conversation requires talking and listening. As I talk to Jesus may I also learn to be still and listen. I picture the gentleness in his eyes and the smile full of love as he gazes on me. I can be totally honest with Jesus as I tell him of my worries and my cares. I will open up my heart to him as I tell him of my fears and my doubts. I will ask him to help me to place myself fully in his care, to abandon myself to him, knowing that he always wants what is best for me.

Conclusion
I thank God for these few moments we have spent alone together and for any insights I may have been given concerning the text.

Sunday 28th February
Third Sunday of Lent
Luke 13:1–9

At that very time there were some present who told him about the Galileans whose blood Pilate had mingled with their sacrifices. He asked them, "Do you think that because these Galileans suffered in this way they were worse sinners than all other Galileans? No, I tell you; but unless you repent, you will all perish as they did. Or those eighteen who were killed when the tower of Siloam fell on them—do you think that they were worse offenders than all the others living in Jerusalem? No, I tell you; but unless you repent, you will all perish just as they did." Then he told this parable: "A man had a fig tree planted in his vineyard; and he came looking for fruit on it and found none. So he said to the gardener, 'See here! For three years I have come looking for fruit on this fig tree, and still I find none. Cut it down! Why should it be wasting the soil?' He replied, 'Sir, let it alone for one more year, until I dig round it and put manure on it. If it bears fruit next year, well and good; but if not, you can cut it down.'"

• Jesus comments on the news stories of his time. Just as in our time, narratives of destruction and distress capture the attention. As always, Jesus is telling us not only to look outward but to look inward as well; he is concerned with what is going on in our heads and what is happening in our hearts. We can ask ourselves how God is opening us to compassion, prompting us to repentance and leading us to life.

- Jesus often speaks of the need to repent. This means turning away from anything that is not of God. I ask to be brought more and more into the world of goodness and love, of light and truth. I want to be a genuine disciple.

Monday 29th February
Luke 4:24–30

Jesus said, "Truly I tell you, no prophet is accepted in the prophet's hometown. But the truth is, there were many widows in Israel in the time of Elijah, when the heaven was shut up three years and six months, and there was a severe famine over all the land; yet Elijah was sent to none of them except to a widow at Zarephath in Sidon. There were also many lepers in Israel in the time of the prophet Elisha, and none of them was cleansed except Naaman the Syrian." When they heard this, all in the synagogue were filled with rage. They got up, drove him out of the town, and led him to the brow of the hill on which their town was built, so that they might hurl him off the cliff. But he passed through the midst of them and went on his way.

- The people in question here were jealous of their community of faith. Jesus was including all nationalities in the care and the saving love of God. They were jealous of their own relationship with God, and used it in many ordinary ways to keep others out of favor and off of land and to deny human rights to anyone outside their circle. Jesus is the one of universal welcome, his heart open in prayer and life to all, no matter their creed, nation, gender, age, or any of the categories with which we are divided from each other.

- When I hear things that hurt my pride, do I attack the speakers and drive them away? Lord, let me be more humble. Let me seek to know the truth about myself, even though it may be painful. Only the truth will set me free.

Tuesday 1st March
Matthew 18:21–35

Peter came and said to him, "Lord, if another member of the church sins against me, how often should I forgive? As many as seven times?" Jesus said to him, "Not seven times, but, I tell you, seventy-seven times. For this reason the kingdom of heaven may be compared to a king who wished to settle accounts with his slaves. When he began the reckoning, one who owed him ten thousand talents was brought to him;

and, as he could not pay, his lord ordered him to be sold, together with his wife and children and all his possessions, and payment to be made. So the slave fell on his knees before him, saying, 'Have patience with me, and I will pay you everything.' And out of pity for him, the lord of that slave released him and forgave him the debt. But that same slave, as he went out, came upon one of his fellow slaves who owed him a hundred denarii; and seizing him by the throat, he said, 'Pay what you owe.' Then his fellow slave fell down and pleaded with him, 'Have patience with me, and I will pay you.' But he refused; then he went and threw him into prison until he would pay the debt. When his fellow slaves saw what had happened, they were greatly distressed, and they went and reported to their lord all that had taken place. Then his lord summoned him and said to him, 'You wicked slave! I forgave you all that debt because you pleaded with me. Should you not have had mercy on your fellow slave, as I had mercy on you?' And in anger his lord handed him over to be tortured until he would pay his entire debt. So my heavenly Father will also do to every one of you, if you do not forgive your brother or sister from your heart."

- I should take some time to try and see how the call to forgiveness affects me. This is a hard one: Forgive and go on forgiving. It means letting go of my treasured grievances and resentments. They are a burden on me, not on the one I resent. In the Lord's Prayer, Jesus makes forgiveness as central as our daily bread. Nothing sets apart the spirit of Christ from other spirits more clearly than this.

- If we must be prepared to forgive seventy-seven times, then we must also be ready to ask for forgiveness—and believe we are forgiven—seventy-seven times. Does forgiveness flow back and forth in my dealings with others, or is it rare in my life?

Wednesday 2nd March
Matthew 5:17–19

Jesus said to his disciples, "Do not think that I have come to abolish the law or the prophets; I have come not to abolish but to fulfill. For truly I tell you, until heaven and earth pass away, not one letter, not one stroke of a letter, will pass from the law until all is accomplished. Therefore, whoever breaks one of the least of these commandments, and teaches others to do the same, will be called least in the kingdom of heaven; but whoever does them and teaches them will be called great in the kingdom of heaven. For I tell you, unless your righteousness exceeds that of the scribes and Pharisees, you will never enter the kingdom of heaven."

- Jesus is not careless about the requirements of the law. He wants us, too, to be attentive and careful and asks us to bring all aspects of our lives before God. I pray that I might respect the voice of my conscience as I try to hear how God is speaking to me.

- I am often told who are the winners and losers; I hear about the great, and I am taught to ignore the small. Jesus shows me a different way of thinking about who is great in his sight. I think of the people I admire and ask Jesus to show me who really deserves my attention.

Thursday 3rd March
Luke 11:14–23

Now Jesus was casting out a demon that was mute; when the demon had gone out, the one who had been mute spoke, and the crowds were amazed. But some of them said, "He casts out demons by Beelzebul, the ruler of the demons." Others, to test him, kept demanding from him a sign from heaven. But he knew what they were thinking and said to them, "Every kingdom divided against itself becomes a desert, and house falls on house. If Satan also is divided against himself, how will his kingdom stand?—for you say that I cast out the demons by Beelzebul. Now if I cast out the demons by Beelzebul, by whom do your exorcists cast them out? Therefore they will be your judges. But if it is by the finger of God that I cast out the demons, then the kingdom of God has come to you. When a strong man, fully armed, guards his castle, his property is safe. But when one stronger than he attacks him and overpowers him, he takes away his armor in which he trusted and divides his plunder. Whoever is not with me is against me, and whoever does not gather with me scatters."

- Some of the original listeners to this story, who have just witnessed Jesus curing a man who was mute, refuse to think well of him and invent a slanderous story. It prods me: Do I think ill of others more readily than I credit them with good? Lord, give me the grace to see the best in others, as I'd wish them to see the best in me.

- Am I divided against myself—sometimes listening to Jesus, sometimes listening to evil? Have I a discerning heart?

Friday 4th March
Mark 12:28–34

One of the scribes came near and heard them disputing with one another, and seeing that Jesus answered them well, he asked him, "Which commandment is the first of all?" Jesus answered, "The first is, 'Hear, O Israel: the Lord our God, the Lord is one; you shall love the Lord your God with all your heart, and with all your soul, and with all your mind, and with all your strength.' The second is this, 'You shall love your neighbor as yourself.' There is no other commandment greater than these." Then the scribe said to him, "You are right, Teacher; you have truly said that 'he is one, and besides him there is no other'; and 'to love him with all the heart, and with all the understanding, and with all the strength,' and 'to love one's neighbor as oneself'—this is much more important than all whole burnt offerings and sacrifices." When Jesus saw that he answered wisely, he said to him, "You are not far from the kingdom of God." After that no one dared to ask him any question.

- Real prayer brings us into the kingdom of God; in prayer the kingdom or reign of God grows within us. Prayer that does not reach the heart can leave us dry, unenthusiastic about the things of God, and dissatisfied.

- "The Lord our God, the Lord is one . . ." As I hear Jesus' answer to the scribe, I think how a Muslim would agree warmly with all that he hears and how Jesus might well say of many a Muslim, Jew, and Christian equally: "You are not far from the kingdom of God." Lord, let me not put barriers where you put windows.

Saturday 5th March

Luke 18:9–14

Jesus also told this parable to some who trusted in themselves that they were righteous and regarded others with contempt: "Two men went up to the temple to pray, one a Pharisee and the other a tax collector. The Pharisee, standing by himself, was praying thus, 'God, I thank you that I am not like other people: thieves, rogues, adulterers, or even like this tax collector. I fast twice a week; I give a tenth of all my income.' But the tax collector, standing far off, would not even look up to heaven, but was beating his breast and saying, 'God, be merciful to me, a sinner!' I tell you, this man went down to his home justified rather than the other; for all who exalt themselves will be humbled, but all who humble themselves will be exalted."

- The contrast between the Pharisee and tax collector has entered so deeply into our culture that it is sometimes reversed, and people are more anxious to hide at the back of the church than to be in the front pews.

- How does the story strike me? I would hate to be the object of people's contempt. But Lord, if they knew me as you do, they might be right to feel contempt. And I have no right to look down on those whose sins are paraded in the media. Be merciful to me.

The Fourth Week of Lent
March 6—March 12

Something to think and pray about each day this week:

Indiscriminate Loving

"God is love in the same way as an emerald is green." So says Simone Weil. What does this mean? It means that God *is* love through and through. There isn't something else hidden behind God's love. Nothing I do could make God love me more—or less! Jesus compares his Father to the sun, which simply shines, so that both the just and the unjust are warmed by it. Every time I see the sun, I can say, "God is a bit like that!"

The task of the Son is to reveal the generous nature of divine loving and then to show people a new way of relating. "Be loving, as my Father and I are loving!" he says. Jesus illustrates in word and deed this new way of relating. His parables jolted and disconcerted his hearers. What a shock that the good neighbor to the injured man was a Samaritan! And surely the good father should have disowned his wayward son? Surely again those who labored all day should get more than the last-minute arrivals?

Jesus had a well-integrated personality. He could be gentle but also challenging and angry. So he clashed head-on with the religious leaders of the day and threw the moneylenders out of the temple. Wise love takes many forms: it is not timid and passive; it can be demanding as well as long-suffering.

The Presence of God
I pause for a moment and think of the love and the grace that God showers on me: I am created in the image and likeness of God; I am God's dwelling place.

Freedom
Lord, you granted me the great gift of freedom. In these times grant that I may be free from any form of racism or intolerance. Remind me, Lord, that we are all equal in your loving eyes.

Consciousness
Knowing that God loves me unconditionally, I can afford to be honest about how I am. How has the past day been, and how do I feel now? I share my feelings openly with the Lord.

The Word
I read the Word of God slowly, a few times over, and I listen to what God is saying to me. (Please turn to the Scripture on the following pages. Inspiration points are provided should you need them. When you are ready, return here to continue.)

Conversation

Jesus, you always welcomed little children when you walked on this earth. Teach me to have a childlike trust in you, to live in the knowledge that you will never abandon me.

Conclusion

Glory be to the Father, and to the Son, and to the Holy Spirit, as it was in the beginning, is now and ever shall be, world without end. Amen.

Sunday 6th March
Fourth Sunday of Lent

Luke 15:1–3, 11–32

Now all the tax collectors and sinners were coming near to listen to him. And the Pharisees and the scribes were grumbling and saying, "This fellow welcomes sinners and eats with them." So he told them this parable: "There was a man who had two sons. The younger of them said to his father, 'Father, give me the share of the property that will belong to me.' So he divided his property between them. A few days later the younger son gathered all he had and traveled to a distant country, and there he squandered his property in dissolute living. When he had spent everything, a severe famine took place throughout that country, and he began to be in need. So he went and hired himself out to one of the citizens of that country, who sent him to his fields to feed the pigs. He would gladly have filled himself with the pods that the pigs were eating; and no one gave him anything. But when he came to himself he said, 'How many of my father's hired hands have bread enough and to spare, but here I am dying of hunger! I will get up and go to my father, and I will say to him, "Father, I have sinned against heaven and before you; I am no longer worthy to be called your son; treat me like one of your hired hands."' So he set off and went to his father. But while he was still far off, his father saw him and was filled with compassion; he ran and put his arms around him and kissed him. Then the son said to him, 'Father, I have sinned against heaven and before you; I am no longer worthy to be called your son.' But the father said to his slaves, 'Quickly, bring out a robe—the best one—and put it on him; put a ring on his finger and sandals on his feet. And get the fatted calf and kill it, and let us eat and celebrate; for this son of mine was dead and is alive again; he was lost and is found!' And they began to celebrate. Now his elder son was in the field; and when he came and approached the house, he heard music and dancing. He called one of the slaves and asked what was going on. He replied, 'Your brother has come, and your father has killed the fatted calf, because he has got him back safe and sound.' Then he became angry and refused to go in. His father came out and began to plead with him. But he answered his father, 'Listen! For all these years I have been working like a slave for you, and I have never disobeyed your command; yet you have never given me even a young goat so that I might celebrate with my friends. But when this son of yours came back, who has devoured your property with prostitutes, you killed the fatted calf for him!' Then the father said to him, 'Son, you are always with me, and all that is mine is yours. But we had to celebrate and rejoice, because this brother of yours was dead and has come to life; he was lost and has been found.'"

- So many of Jesus' parables, like this one, startle their hearers with their shocking picture of God's inclusive love—which seeks out one lost sheep, turns a house upside down to find a single coin, and pays those who have worked the least the same as those who have worked the most. Every single person is important to God. Do you feel that way about yourself? Do you treat others with that same awareness?

- The Pharisees and scribes resented Jesus when he dared to welcome sinners. Like the older son in the story, they were insiders, the faithful ones who felt they had earned God's favor. Now they were being asked not to exclude those who had sinned but to rejoice over their repentance. God calls us to look for opportunities to overcome our prejudices and desire to exclude and instead to embrace God's mercy.

Monday 7th March
John 4:43–54

When the two days were over, he went from that place to Galilee (for Jesus himself had testified that a prophet has no honor in the prophet's own country). When he came to Galilee, the Galileans welcomed him, since they had seen all that he had done in Jerusalem at the festival; for they too had gone to the festival. Then he came again to Cana in Galilee where he had changed the water into wine. Now there was a royal official whose son lay ill in Capernaum. When he heard that Jesus had come from Judea to Galilee, he went and begged him to come down and heal his son, for he was at the point of death. Then Jesus said to him, "Unless you see signs and wonders you will not believe." The official said to him, "Sir, come down before my little boy dies." Jesus said to him, "Go; your son will live." The man believed the word that Jesus spoke to him and started on his way. As he was going down, his slaves met him and told him that his child was alive. So he asked them the hour when he began to recover, and they said to him, "Yesterday at one in the afternoon the fever left him." The father realized that this was the hour when Jesus had said to him, "Your son will live." So he himself believed, along with his whole household. Now this was the second sign that Jesus did after coming from Judea to Galilee.

- At first Jesus recoils when the official begs him to cure his son: "Unless you see signs and wonders you will not believe." He is exposed to countless requests for help, but what he treasures most is the company of those—like Martha's sister

Mary—who want to know God for himself, not for what he can deliver. After the child is healed, and the father returns in gratitude and faith, Jesus welcomes him.

• Lord, forgive me for the times I have treated you like a messenger. I turn to you in a crisis, begging for a favor. When the crisis passes, I easily go back to living as though you did not exist. I want to find time for you, to live in your presence.

Tuesday 8th March
John 5:1–16

There was a festival of the Jews, and Jesus went up to Jerusalem. Now in Jerusalem by the Sheep Gate there is a pool, called in Hebrew Beth-zatha, which has five porticoes. In these lay many invalids—blind, lame, and paralyzed. One man was there who had been ill for thirty-eight years. When Jesus saw him lying there and knew that he had been there a long time, he said to him, "Do you want to be made well?" The sick man answered him, "Sir, I have no one to put me into the pool when the water is stirred up; and while I am making my way, someone else steps down ahead of me." Jesus said to him, "Stand up, take your mat and walk." At once the man was made well, and he took up his mat and began to walk. Now that day was a sabbath. So the Jews said to the man who had been cured, "It is the sabbath; it is not lawful for you to carry your mat." But he answered them, "The man who made me well said to me, 'Take up your mat and walk.'" They asked him, "Who is the man who said to you, 'Take it up and walk'?" Now the man who had been healed did not know who it was, for Jesus had disappeared in the crowd that was there. Later Jesus found him in the temple and said to him, "See, you have been made well! Do not sin any more, so that nothing worse happens to you." The man went away and told the Jews that it was Jesus who had made him well. Therefore the Jews started persecuting Jesus, because he was doing such things on the sabbath.

- I can wait all my life for the stirring of the water. How safe it is not to see, not to have to move! No one can blame me for my inaction because there's nobody to lift me. When Jesus asks, "Do you want to be made well?" I don't really answer the question. I am not sure. If I were healed I would have to move on from the familiar place in which I have been lying all these years. God, stir my heart!

- The man by the pool is waiting for healing from the stirring of the waters. He does not know that Jesus, source of all healing, is standing beside him. Do I look for healing in the wrong places?

Wednesday 9th March

John 5:17–30

Jesus answered them, "My Father is still working, and I also am working." For this reason the Jews were seeking all the more to kill him, because he was not only breaking the sabbath, but was also calling God his own Father, thereby making himself equal to God. Jesus said to them, "Very truly, I tell you, the Son can do nothing on his own, but only what he sees the Father doing; for whatever the Father does, the Son does likewise. The Father loves the Son and shows him all that he himself is doing; and he will show him greater works than these, so that you will be astonished. Indeed, just as the Father raises the dead and gives them life, so also the Son gives life to whomsoever he wishes. The Father judges no one but has given all judgment to the Son, so that all may honor the Son just as they honor the Father. Anyone who does not honor the Son does not honor the Father who sent him. Very truly, I tell you, anyone who hears my word and believes him who sent me has eternal life, and does not come under judgment, but has passed from death to life. Very truly, I tell you, the hour is coming, and is now here, when the dead will hear the voice of the Son of God, and those who hear will live. For just as the Father has life in himself, so he has granted the Son also to have life in himself; and he has given him authority to execute judgment, because he is the Son of Man. Do not be astonished at this; for the hour is coming when all who are in their graves will hear his voice and will come out—those who have done good, to the resurrection of life, and those who have done evil, to the resurrection of condemnation. I can do nothing on my own. As I hear, I judge; and my judgment is just, because I seek to do not my own will but the will of him who sent me."

- Jesus is utterly attentive to the Father. This attention allows the Father's creative, life-giving love to flow through Christ to those around him. Perfect love demands perfect attention. How attentive will I be to the people in my life today?

- The relationship between the Father and Son is perfect. The Father is reflected in all that the Son does. Do I bear witness to God's work in what I say and do?

Thursday 10th March
John 5:31–47

Jesus said, "If I testify about myself, my testimony is not true. There is another who testifies on my behalf, and I know that his testimony to me is true. You sent messengers to John, and he testified to the truth. Not that I accept such human testimony, but

I say these things so that you may be saved. He was a burning and shining lamp, and you were willing to rejoice for a while in his light. But I have a testimony greater than John's. The works that the Father has given me to complete, the very works that I am doing, testify on my behalf that the Father has sent me. And the Father who sent me has himself testified on my behalf. You have never heard his voice or seen his form, and you do not have his word abiding in you, because you do not believe him whom he has sent. You search the Scriptures because you think that in them you have eternal life; and it is they that testify on my behalf. Yet you refuse to come to me to have life. I do not accept glory from human beings. But I know that you do not have the love of God in you. I have come in my Father's name, and you do not accept me; if another comes in his own name, you will accept him. How can you believe when you accept glory from one another and do not seek the glory that comes from the one who alone is God? Do not think that I will accuse you before the Father; your accuser is Moses, on whom you have set your hope. If you believed Moses, you would believe me, for he wrote about me. But if you do not believe what he wrote, how will you believe what I say?"

- The biblical rule of evidence required two witnesses. Jesus calls on John the Baptist and Moses to testify to his identity and mission. What would a person of integrity say about me?

- John the Baptist fulfilled Isaiah's prophecy that a voice would cry, "In the wilderness prepare the way of the Lord; make straight in the desert a highway for our God" (Isaiah 40:3). As we make our Lenten journey, let us reflect on what we are doing to make our own crooked ways straight.

Friday 11th March
John 7:1–2, 10, 25–30

Jesus went about in Galilee. He did not wish to go about in Judea because the Jews were looking for an opportunity to kill him. Now the Jewish festival of Booths was near. But after his brothers had gone to the festival, then he also went, not publicly but as it were in secret. Now some of the people of Jerusalem were saying, "Is not this the man whom they are trying to kill? And here he is, speaking openly, but they say nothing to him! Can it be that the authorities really know that this is the Messiah? Yet we know where this man is from; but when the Messiah comes, no one will know where he is from." Then Jesus cried out as he was teaching in the temple, "You know me, and you know where I am from. I have not come on my own. But the one who sent me is true, and you do not know him. I know him, because I am from him, and he sent me." Then they tried to arrest him, but no one laid hands on him, because his hour had not yet come.

- This Gospel passage describes the struggle in Jesus: how to reveal himself to his people when many of them were seeking an excuse to kill him. Because they know he is from Nazareth, they write him off—it is too ordinary a place to produce a Messiah.

- Lord, you show yourself to me in the ordinary. Let me recognize you there today.

Saturday 12th March
John 7:40–53

When they heard Jesus' words, some in the crowd said, "This is really the prophet." Others said, "This is the Messiah." But some asked, "Surely the Messiah does not come from Galilee, does he? Has not the Scripture said that the Messiah is descended from David and comes from Bethlehem, the village where David lived?" So there was a division in the crowd because of him. Some of them wanted to arrest him, but no one laid hands on him. Then the temple police went back to the chief priests and Pharisees, who asked them, "Why did you not arrest him?" The police answered, "Never has anyone spoken like this!" Then the Pharisees replied, "Surely you have not been deceived too, have you? Has any one of the authorities or of the Pharisees believed in him? But this crowd, which does not know the law—they are accursed." Nicodemus, who had gone to Jesus before, and who was one of them, asked, "Our law does not judge people without first giving them a hearing to find out what they are doing, does it?" They replied, "Surely you are not also from Galilee, are you? Search and you will see that no prophet is to arise from Galilee." Then each of them went home.

- Here are two ways of approaching Jesus: some hear him, see how he lives, and love and enjoy him; others go back to their books and argue about his pedigree.

- Lord, save me from losing you in the babble of books and arguments. May I meet and know and enjoy you.

The Fifth Week of Lent
March 13—March 19

Something to think and pray about each day this week:

Wanting to Forgive

If I refuse absolutely even to want to forgive, I cannot pray the Our Father. It makes no sense. But if I have problems with forgiving, then I can pray it. In effect I am saying: "Lord, I have great problems with what you call me to. Please help me. You are better at forgiving than I am, so please forgive me fully, no matter how I hurt you. I accept that you want me to keep on trying to forgive, and I will try."

So the divine call to forgive is addressed to me as I am, in my actual situation. I am called to do what I can, no more, no less. But I know that the love of Christ is always inviting me beyond where I am. On that difficult journey toward loving our enemy, we have a friend in our Lord, not another enemy throwing even more burdens on us. Because he is our friend, he is not going to be shocked at our feelings of anger or revenge. He will understand these, because he shares our anger and horror at what has been done to us. He will walk with us as we move slowly toward freedom, where we are no longer dominated by what has happened to us.

The Presence of God
Come to me all you who are burdened, and I will give you rest. Here I am, Lord. I come to seek your presence. I long for your healing power.

Freedom
Lord grant me the grace to have freedom of the spirit. Cleanse my heart and soul so I may live joyously in your love.

Consciousness
Knowing that God loves me unconditionally, I look honestly over the last day, its events and my feelings. Do I have something to be grateful for? Then I give thanks. Is there something I am sorry for? Then I ask forgiveness.

The Word
God speaks to each one of us individually. I listen attentively to hear what he is saying to me. Read the text a few times, then listen. (Please turn to the Scripture on the following pages. Inspiration points are provided should you need them. When you are ready, return here to continue.)

Conversation
Remembering that I am still in God's presence, I imagine Jesus himself standing or sitting beside me,

and I say whatever is on my mind, whatever is in my heart, speaking as one friend to another.

Conclusion

I thank God for these few moments we have spent alone together and for any insights I may have been given concerning the text.

Sunday 13th March
Fifth Sunday of Lent

John 8:1–11

Early in the morning Jesus came again to the temple. All the people came to him and he sat down and began to teach them. The scribes and the Pharisees brought a woman who had been caught in adultery; and making her stand before all of them, they said to him, "Teacher, this woman was caught in the very act of committing adultery. Now in the law Moses commanded us to stone such women. Now what do you say?" They said this to test him, so that they might have some charge to bring against him. Jesus bent down and wrote with his finger on the ground. When they kept on questioning him, he straightened up and said to them, "Let anyone among you who is without sin be the first to throw a stone at her." And once again he bent down and wrote on the ground. When they heard it, they went away, one by one, beginning with the elders; and Jesus was left alone with the woman standing before him. Jesus straightened up and said to her, "Woman, where are they? Has no one condemned you?" She said, "No one, sir." And Jesus said, "Neither do I condemn you. Go your way, and from now on do not sin again.'"

- Where do I stand in this scene? Like the woman standing before her accusers? Like a silent sympathizer hoping that something will happen to save her? Like the skulking male adulterer who got her into this trouble? Like the bystanders already collecting the best stones with a view to a killing? Like one of the elders who slinks away, unable to cast the first stone? What goes through my head as Jesus is doodling in the sand?

- Sometimes we are overwhelmed by a sense of our own guilt. The voices of accusation roar in our ears. Frozen with fear, we wait for condemnation. Lord, like the woman in the reading, may we hear the damning voices fade until there is only your voice left, telling us to move on and sin no more.

Monday 14th March
John 8:12–20

Again Jesus spoke to them, saying, "I am the light of the world. Whoever follows me will never walk in darkness but will have the light of life." Then the Pharisees said to him, "You are testifying on your own behalf; your testimony is not valid." Jesus answered, "Even if I testify on my own behalf, my testimony is valid because I know where I have come from and where I am going, but you do not know where I come from or where I am going. You judge by human standards; I judge no one. Yet even if I do judge, my judgment is valid; for it is not I alone who judge, but I and the Father who sent me. In your law it is written that the testimony of two witnesses is valid. I testify on my own behalf, and the Father who sent me testifies on my behalf." Then they said to him, "Where is your Father?" Jesus answered, "You know neither me nor my Father. If you knew me, you would know my Father also." He spoke these words while he was teaching in the treasury of the temple, but no one arrested him, because his hour had not yet come.

- On the first day of creation God flooded the heavens and the earth with divine radiance by uttering the mighty words: "Let there be light." No matter how dark things may seem, I remind myself that darkness can never overpower light. I turn to Christ, the light of the world.

- I pray in the words of Saint Benedict: "O gracious and Holy Father, give us wisdom to perceive you, diligence to seek you, patience to wait for you, eyes to behold you, a heart to meditate upon you, and a life to proclaim you; through the power of the Spirit of Jesus Christ our Lord."

Tuesday 15th March
John 8:21–30

Jesus said to them, "I am going away, and you will search for me, but you will die in your sin. Where

I am going, you cannot come." Then the Jews said, "Is he going to kill himself? Is that what he means by saying, 'Where I am going, you cannot come'?" He said to them, "You are from below, I am from above; you are of this world, I am not of this world. I told you that you would die in your sins, for you will die in your sins unless you believe that I am he." They said to him, "Who are you?" Jesus said to them, "Why do I speak to you at all? I have much to say about you and much to condemn; but the one who sent me is true, and I declare to the world what I have heard from him." They did not understand that he was speaking to them about the Father. So Jesus said, "When you have lifted up the Son of Man, then you will realize that I am he, and that I do nothing on my own, but I speak these things as the Father instructed me. And the one who sent me is with me; he has not let me alone, for I always do what is pleasing to him." As he was saying these things, many believed in him.

- In the days of Jesus' Passion we hear him crying out to God in doubt. He might remember these words he spoke, that God does not leave him alone. We, too, are never alone; the love, grace, and help of God are always with us. Give thanks in prayer for these gifts or ask for what you need just now.

- It is when we see Jesus lifted up on the cross that we realize who he is and why he lived. The rest of the Gospels are like a preface to the Passion. On the cross we see the triumph of love over evil, and our best help in coping with the reality of evil.

Wednesday 16th March

John 8:31–42

Then Jesus said to the Jews who had believed in him, "If you continue in my word, you are truly my disciples; and you will know the truth, and the truth will make you free." They answered him, "We are descendants of Abraham and have never been slaves to anyone. What do you mean by saying, 'You will be made free'?" Jesus answered them, "Very truly, I tell you, everyone who commits sin is a slave to sin. The slave does not have a permanent place in the household; the Son has a place there forever. So if the Son makes you free, you will be free indeed. I know that you are descendants of Abraham; yet you look for an opportunity to kill me, because there is no place in you for my word. I declare what I have seen in the Father's presence; as for you, you should do what you have heard from the Father." They answered him, "Abraham is our father." Jesus said to them, "If you were Abraham's children, you would be doing what Abraham did, but now you are trying to kill me, a man who has told you the truth that I heard from God. This is not what Abraham did. You are indeed doing what your father does." They said to him, "We are not illegitimate children; we have one father, God himself." Jesus said to them, "If God were your Father, you would love me, for I came from God and now I am here. I did not come on my own, but he sent me."

- Jesus' promise is that the truth will make us free. Lord, I do want to be free, so let me listen to those who tell me the truth about myself. Let me listen also to your word, which tries to reach into my heart and liberate me. Let me start with the great truth of which you try to convince me: that I am endlessly loved by you.

- When in my life have I had an experience that made me truly see Jesus as the one sent by God?

Thursday 17th March
John 8:51–59

Jesus said, "Very truly, I tell you, whoever keeps my word will never see death." The Jews said to him, "Now we know that you have a demon. Abraham died, and so did the prophets; yet you say, 'Whoever keeps my word will never taste death.' Are you greater than our father Abraham, who died? The prophets also died. Who do you claim to be?" Jesus answered,

"If I glorify myself, my glory is nothing. It is my Father who glorifies me, he of whom you say, 'He is our God,' though you do not know him. But I know him; if I were to say that I do not know him, I would be a liar like you. But I do know him and I keep his word. Your ancestor Abraham rejoiced that he would see my day; he saw it and was glad." Then the Jews said to him, "You are not yet fifty years old, and have you seen Abraham?" Jesus said to them, "Very truly, I tell you, before Abraham was, I am." So they picked up stones to throw at him, but Jesus hid himself and went out of the temple.

- The Jews had no doubt that Jesus was claiming a divine nature. As son of Mary he was born in Bethlehem in time; but as God he is outside time—the same yesterday, today, and forever.

- Lord I am praying here on the edge of what I can grasp, reaching for the eternal Now. What matters to me is that you are as much my contemporary as you were of Pilate and the stone-throwing enemies of Jesus.

Friday 18th March
John 10:31–42

The Jews took up stones again to stone him. Jesus replied, "I have shown you many good works from the Father. For which of these are you going to stone me?"

The Jews answered, "It is not for a good work that we are going to stone you, but for blasphemy, because you, though only a human being, are making yourself God." Jesus answered, "Is it not written in your law, 'I said, you are gods'? If those to whom the Word of God came were called 'gods'—and the Scripture cannot be annulled—can you say that the one whom the Father has sanctified and sent into the world is blaspheming because I said, 'I am God's Son'? If I am not doing the works of my Father, then do not believe me. But if I do them, even though you do not believe me, believe the works, so that you may know and understand that the Father is in me and I am in the Father." Then they tried to arrest him again, but he escaped from their hands. He went away again across the Jordan to the place where John had been baptizing earlier, and he remained there. Many came to him, and they were saying, "John performed no sign, but everything that John said about this man was true." And many believed in him there.

- The works of Jesus are the works of love. This is the love of him we know—love unto death. What we see in Jesus we can see of the Father. What the Father sees in Jesus, he sees and loves in us. We pray that our hearts may be made like the heart of Jesus.

- Some believed in Jesus, and some did not. In a way that's the basic question the Gospel puts to us, too. Do we really believe that in Jesus we see God? And if we believe in Jesus, can others recognize Jesus in us?

Saturday 19th March
Saint Joseph, Spouse of the Blessed Virgin Mary
Matthew 1:16, 18–21, 24a

Jacob [was] the father of Joseph the husband of Mary, of whom Jesus was born, who is called the Messiah. Now the birth of Jesus the Messiah took place in this way. When his mother Mary had been engaged to Joseph, but before they lived together, she was found to be with child from the Holy Spirit. Her husband Joseph, being a righteous man and unwilling to expose her to public disgrace, planned to dismiss her quietly. But just when he had resolved to do this, an angel of the Lord appeared to him in a dream and said, "Joseph, son of David, do not be afraid to take Mary as your wife, for the child conceived in her is from the Holy Spirit. She will bear a son, and you are to name him Jesus, for he will save his people from their sins." When Joseph awoke from sleep, he did as the angel of the Lord commanded him; he took her as his wife.

- What do we know about Saint Joseph? That he loved Mary so much that he suppressed his doubts about her chastity and allowed himself to be regarded as the father of her child, knowing that he wasn't; that he brought up that child as his own, despite great difficulties and dangers, particularly at the start; that he taught him his trade; that he loved him; and that his parenting, evident in Jesus' virile health as an adult (physical stamina, courage, strength of purpose, and appeal to women, men, and children), was good and successful. Joseph is the obvious patron of adoptive fathers of all kinds.

- God, you give your help and guidance to those who trust in you. Where do I need your help and guidance today?

March 20—March 26

Something to think and pray about each day this week:

Suffering and Joy

In the culture of Jesus' time, crucifixion was a disgraceful way to die. So it took time for the disciples to see in this dreadful event the supreme revelation of God's love for us. We must never trivialize or domesticate this enduring shock. The cross remains, to convert us to God's way of seeing the appalling damage caused by sin and evil. We learn how demanding reconciliation is. Amazing grace is revealed, but it is costly grace, too. It seemed to Jesus that only the cross would break open our hearts, so it was worth it. That hope brought him joy.

We are asked to suffer, if necessary, in order to foster the values of the kingdom. As followers of Jesus we, too, must be in solidarity with a wounded humanity. This may mean living simply for the sake of others; or working with the sick; or spending time with life's victims. For all of us it means enduring with patience the day-to-day difficulties of life.

Suffering is often unearned and always undesired: often we can't change it, but Jesus shows us how to bear it with love. Such love radiates and inspires others. You know such people, and perhaps you are this way yourself without feeling in any way heroic. Mysteriously, joy is possible even in suffering, perhaps because suffering brings us so close to God.

The Presence of God
The more we call on God, the more we can feel God's presence. Day by day we are drawn closer to the loving heart of God.

Freedom
Your death on the cross has set me free. I can live joyously and freely without fear of death. Your mercy knows no bounds.

Consciousness
I remind myself that I am in the presence of the Lord. I will take refuge in his loving heart. He is my strength in times of weakness. He is my comforter in times of sorrow.

The Word
I take my time to read the Word of God slowly, a few times, allowing myself to dwell on anything that strikes me. (Please turn to the Scripture on the following pages. Inspiration points are provided should you need them. When you are ready, return here to continue.)

Conversation

Do I notice myself reacting as I pray with the Word of God? Do I feel challenged, comforted, angry? Imagining Jesus sitting or standing by me, I speak out my feelings, as one trusted friend to another.

Conclusion

Glory be to the Father, and to the Son, and to the Holy Spirit, as it was in the beginning, is now and ever shall be, world without end. Amen.

Sunday 20th March
Palm Sunday of the Passion of the Lord
Luke 23:1–49

Then the assembly rose as a body and brought Jesus before Pilate. They began to accuse him, saying, "We found this man perverting our nation, forbidding us to pay taxes to the emperor, and saying that he himself is the Messiah, a king." Then Pilate asked him, "Are you the king of the Jews?" He answered, "You say so." Then Pilate said to the chief priests and the crowds, "I find no basis for an accusation against this man." But they were insistent and said, "He stirs up the people by teaching throughout all Judea, from Galilee where he began even to this place." When Pilate heard this, he asked whether the man was a Galilean. And when he learned that he was under Herod's jurisdiction, he sent him off to Herod, who was himself in Jerusalem at that time. When Herod saw Jesus, he was very glad, for he had been wanting to see him for a long time, because he had heard about him and was hoping to see him perform some sign. He questioned him at some length, but Jesus gave him no answer. The chief priests and the scribes stood by, vehemently accusing him. Even Herod with his soldiers treated him with contempt and mocked him; then he put an elegant robe on him, and sent him back to Pilate. That same day Herod and Pilate became friends with each other; before this they had been enemies. Pilate then called together the chief priests, the leaders, and the people, and said to them, "You brought me this man as one who was perverting the people; and here I have examined him in your presence and have not found this man guilty of any of your charges against him. Neither has Herod, for he sent him back to us. Indeed, he has done nothing to deserve death. I will therefore have him flogged and release him." Then they all shouted out together, "Away with this fellow! Release Barabbas for us!" (This was a man who had been put in prison for an insurrection that had taken place in the city, and for murder.) Pilate, wanting to release Jesus, addressed them again; but they kept shouting, "Crucify, crucify him!" A third time he said to them, "Why, what evil has he done? I have found in him no ground for the sentence of death; I will therefore have him flogged and then release him." But they kept urgently demanding with loud shouts that he should be crucified; and their voices prevailed. So Pilate gave his verdict that their demand should be granted. He released the man they asked for, the one who had been put in prison for insurrection and murder, and he handed Jesus over as they wished. As they led him away, they seized a man, Simon of Cyrene, who was coming from the country, and they laid the cross on him, and made him carry it behind Jesus. A great number of the people followed him, and among them were women who were beating their breasts and wailing for him. But Jesus turned to them and said, "Daughters of Jerusalem, do not weep for me, but weep for yourselves and for your children. For the days are surely coming when they will say, 'Blessed are the barren, and the wombs that never bore, and the breasts that never nursed.' Then they will begin to say to the mountains, 'Fall on us'; and to the hills, 'Cover us.' For if they do this when the wood is green, what will happen when it is dry?" Two others also, who were criminals, were led away to be put to death with him. When they came to the place that is called the Skull, they crucified Jesus there with the criminals, one on his right and one on his left. Then Jesus said, "Father, forgive them; for they do not know what they are doing." And they cast lots to divide his clothing. And the people stood by, watching; but the leaders scoffed at him, saying, "He saved others; let him save himself if he is the Messiah of God, his chosen one!" The soldiers also mocked him, coming up and offering him sour wine, and saying, "If you are the King of the Jews, save yourself!" There was also an inscription over him, "This is the King of the Jews." One of the criminals who were hanged there kept deriding him and saying, "Are you not the Messiah? Save yourself and us!" But the other rebuked him, saying, "Do you not fear God, since you are under the same sentence of condemnation?

And we indeed have been condemned justly, for we are getting what we deserve for our deeds, but this man has done nothing wrong." Then he said, "Jesus, remember me when you come into your kingdom." He replied, "Truly I tell you, today you will be with me in Paradise." It was now about noon, and darkness came over the whole land until three in the afternoon, while the sun's light failed; and the curtain of the temple was torn in two. Then Jesus, crying with a loud voice, said, "Father, into your hands I commend my spirit." Having said this, he breathed his last. When the centurion saw what had taken place, he praised God and said, "Certainly this man was innocent." And when all the crowds who had gathered there for this spectacle saw what had taken place, they returned home, beating their breasts. But all his acquaintances, including the women who had followed him from Galilee, stood at a distance, watching these things.

- We need to train ourselves to look for signs of Jesus' reign. His real identity can be seen only by the humble. The "good thief" saw things as they were: he knew his own sinfulness; he recognized Jesus' character; he asked for little yet was rewarded for his honesty. Humility brings a true perspective and is the ground for meeting God. I pray for humility.

- In the extraordinary mystery of the Eucharist, Lord, you become part of me and I of you. I celebrate this Eucharist in memory of you: slake my hunger and thirst on the bread and wine and through this come closest to meeting my deepest desire, for union with God.

Monday 21st March

John 12:1–11

Six days before the Passover Jesus came to Bethany, the home of Lazarus, whom he had raised from the dead. There they gave a dinner for him. Martha served, and Lazarus was one of those at the table with him. Mary took a pound of costly perfume made of pure nard, anointed Jesus' feet, and wiped them with her hair. The house was filled with the fragrance of the perfume. But Judas Iscariot, one of his disciples (the one who was about to betray him), said, "Why was this perfume not sold for three hundred denarii and the money given to the poor?" (He said this not because he cared about the poor, but because he was a thief; he kept the common purse and used to steal what was put into it.) Jesus said, "Leave her alone. She bought it so that she might keep it for the day of my burial. You always have the poor with you, but you do not always have me." When the great crowd of the Jews learned that he was there, they came not only because of Jesus but also to see Lazarus, whom he had raised from the dead. So the chief priests planned to put Lazarus to death as well, since it was on account of him that many of the Jews were deserting and were believing in Jesus.

- The gift of Mary: the most costly gift she could find. Jesus was open-hearted enough to receive her gift even though others would need the money spent on it. What is my gift to give him this day as I pray? Offer the gift of your loving heart.

- Lord, when I find myself critical of others, it may be my own warped vision that needs to be corrected.

Tuesday 22nd March
John 13:21–33, 36–38

Jesus was troubled in spirit, and declared, "Very truly, I tell you, one of you will betray me." The disciples looked at one another, uncertain of whom he was speaking. One of his disciples—the one whom Jesus loved—was reclining next to him; Simon Peter therefore motioned to him to ask Jesus of whom he was speaking. So while reclining next to Jesus, he asked him, "Lord, who is it?" Jesus answered, "It is the one to whom I give this piece of bread when I have dipped it in the dish." So when he had dipped the piece of bread, he gave it to Judas son of Simon Iscariot. After he received the piece of bread, Satan entered into him. Jesus said to him, "Do quickly what you are going to do." Now no one at the table knew why he said this to him. Some thought that, because Judas had the common purse, Jesus was telling him, "Buy what we need for the festival"; or, that he should give something to the poor. So, after receiving the piece of bread, he immediately went out. And it was night. When he had gone out, Jesus said, "Now the Son of Man has been glorified, and God has been glorified in him. If God has been glorified in him, God will also glorify him in himself and will glorify him at once. Little children, I am with you only a little longer. You will look for me; and as I said to the Jews so now I say to you, 'Where I am going, you cannot come.'" Simon Peter said to him, "Lord, where are you going?" Jesus answered, "Where I am going, you cannot follow me now; but you will follow afterward." Peter said to him, "Lord, why can I not follow you now? I will lay down my life for you." Jesus answered, "Will you lay down your life for me? Very truly, I tell you, before the cock crows, you will have denied me three times."

- God is glorified in all sorts of ways. He is glorified in the Passion of Jesus, as all that is done is done from love. Even in sending out Judas there is the beginning of the journey of passion—love that will result in the love of the cross.

- Peter hit deep points of his life here. His sureness of following Jesus was challenged by Jesus himself. He would later find himself weak and failing in this following. We oscillate in our following of the Lord; these days let us know in the certainty of Jesus' love that there is always another day, another chance, another joy in our following of Jesus.

Wednesday 23rd March
Matthew 26:14–25

Then one of the twelve, who was called Judas Iscariot, went to the chief priests and said, "What will you give me if I betray him to you?" They paid him thirty pieces of silver. And from that moment he began to look for an opportunity to betray him. On the first day of Unleavened Bread the disciples came to Jesus, saying, "Where do you want us to make the preparations for you to eat the Passover?" He said, "Go into the city to a certain man, and say to him, 'The Teacher says, My time is near; I will keep the Passover at your house with my disciples.'" So the disciples did as Jesus had directed them, and they prepared the Passover meal. When it was evening, he took his place with the twelve; and while they were eating, he said, "Truly I tell you, one of you will betray me." And they became greatly distressed and began to say to him one after another, "Surely not I,

Lord?" He answered, "The one who has dipped his hand into the bowl with me will betray me. The Son of Man goes as it is written of him, but woe to that one by whom the Son of Man is betrayed! It would have been better for that one not to have been born." Judas, who betrayed him, said, "Surely not I, Rabbi?" He replied, "You have said so."

- Holy Week is an invitation to walk closely with Jesus: we fix our gaze on him and accompany him in his suffering; we let him look closely at us and see us as we really are. We do not have to present a brave face to him but can tell him about where we have been disappointed, let down—perhaps even betrayed. We avoid getting stuck in our own misfortune by seeing as he sees, by learning from his heart.

- Help me to see, Jesus, how you do not condemn. You invite each of us to recognize the truth of our own discipleship. You invite us to follow you willingly, freely, forgiven.

Thursday 24th March
Holy Thursday
John 13:1–15

Now before the festival of the Passover, Jesus knew that his hour had come to depart from this world and go to the Father. Having loved his own who were in the world, he loved them to the end. The devil had already put it into the heart of Judas son of Simon Iscariot to betray him. And during supper Jesus, knowing that the Father had given all things into his hands, and that he had come from God and was going to God, got up from the table, took off his outer robe, and tied a towel around himself. Then he poured water into a basin and began to wash the disciples' feet and to wipe them with the towel that was tied around him. He came to Simon Peter, who said to him, "Lord, are you going to wash my feet?" Jesus answered, "You do not know now what I am doing, but later you will understand." Peter said to him, "You will never wash my feet." Jesus answered, "Unless I wash you, you have no share with me." Simon Peter said to him, "Lord, not my feet only but also my hands and my head!" Jesus said to him, "One who has bathed does not need to wash, except for the feet, but is entirely clean. And you are clean, though not all of you." For he knew who was to betray him; for this reason he said, "Not all of you are clean." After he had washed their feet, had put on his robe, and had returned to the table, he said to them, "Do you know what I have done to you? You call me Teacher and Lord—and you are right, for that is what I am. So if I, your Lord and Teacher, have washed your feet, you also ought to wash one another's feet. For I have set you an example, that you also should do as I have done to you."

- Can you watch this scene and allow Jesus to wash your feet? Imagine him looking at you, pouring water, and drying your feet. This is what he wants to do. Allow him! And then maybe you might imagine yourself doing the same for others. As you do this, pray for them.

- Jesus says, "Later you will understand." Sometimes that's not enough for me! I want to understand now. Help me, Jesus, to live as you did even when I don't fully comprehend what you are asking of me.

Friday 25th March
Friday of the Passion of the Lord (Good Friday)
John 18:1—19:24

Pilate handed Jesus over to them to be crucified. So they took Jesus; and carrying the cross by himself, he went out to what is called the Place of the Skull, which in Hebrew is called Golgotha. There they crucified him, and with him two others, one on either side, with Jesus between them. Pilate also had an inscription written and put on the cross. It read, "Jesus of Nazareth, the King of the Jews." Many of the Jews read this inscription, because the place where Jesus was crucified was near the city; and it was written in Hebrew, in Latin, and in Greek. Then the chief priests of the Jews said to Pilate, "Do not write, 'The

King of the Jews,' but, 'This man said, I am King of the Jews.'" Pilate answered, "What I have written I have written." When the soldiers had crucified Jesus, they took his clothes and divided them into four parts, one for each soldier. They also took his tunic; now the tunic was seamless, woven in one piece from the top. So they said to one another, "Let us not tear it, but cast lots for it to see who will get it." This was to fulfill what the Scripture says, "They divided my clothes among themselves, and for my clothing they cast lots."

- Can you look at the cross and allow Jesus to die for you? Notice how you feel and what you would like to say. Maybe the questions of Saint Ignatius of Loyola in looking at the crucified Christ come to mind: "What have I done for Christ? What am I doing for Christ? What ought I to do for Christ?"

- Good Friday puts the cross before me and challenges me not to look away. If I have followed Jesus' footsteps to Calvary, I do not have to fear because I, like him, am confident in God's enduring presence. Wherever there is suffering or pain, I look again, seeking the face of Jesus. I ask him for the strength I need to be a sign of hope wherever there is despair, to be a presence of love wherever it is most needed.

Saturday 26th March
Holy Saturday
Luke 24:1–12

On the first day of the week, at early dawn, they came to the tomb, taking the spices that they had prepared. They found the stone rolled away from the tomb, but when they went in, they did not find the body. While they were perplexed about this, suddenly two men in dazzling clothes stood beside them. The women were terrified and bowed their faces to the ground, but the men said to them, "Why do you look for the living among the dead? He is not here, but has risen. Remember how he told you, while he was still in Galilee, that the Son of Man must be handed over to sinners, and be crucified, and on the third day rise again." Then they remembered his words, and returning from the tomb, they told all this to the eleven and to all the rest. Now it was Mary Magdalene, Joanna, Mary the mother of James, and the other women with them who told this to the apostles. But these words seemed to them an idle tale, and they did not believe them. But Peter got up and ran to the tomb; stooping and looking in, he saw the linen cloths by themselves; then he went home, amazed at what had happened.

- We can picture the women moving through the garden with heavy hearts, oblivious to the dawning spring morning. They are oblivious above all to the glorious presence of the risen Christ not a stone's throw away. Lord, help me to realize that when I am weighed down with sorrow, anxiety, or hopelessness, you are no farther from me than you were from the women in that dawn garden.

• Women are the first witnesses to the resurrection. They reveal the qualities of good disciples in their capacity to believe. I ask not to treat the resurrection as an idle tale but as the message that transforms our world and gives hope to everyone.

Easter Sunday of the Resurrection of the Lord
March 27

Something to think and pray about each day this week:

The Joy of Freedom
We belong to God's own family. How then can we act as if we are still slaves? We can move beyond lives of quiet desperation; we can stop feeling burdened, hopeless, dull, and passive. Our liberation was Jesus' agenda: "The Spirit has sent me to proclaim release to the captives . . . to let the oppressed go free" (Luke 4:18). The liberation of humankind is his great achievement.

Our freedom is God's primary gift to us. In fact it makes us like God. We need not be afraid to claim it and exercise it. Even when we misuse our free will, God does not take it away but works to undo the damage we cause. We learn from Jesus how to use our freedom well. He makes us a free people, a chosen race, sons and daughters of God. How should such people live? Not as slaves or sheep, surely, but as people who had been imprisoned but have just been let out into the open air and the sunlight that the free enjoy.

Of course I have to struggle to grow in freedom. It doesn't happen all at once. But I can make a fresh start every day. I pray: "God, thank you for my freedom. Let me live it out well today. Give me joy, energy, enthusiasm, and commitment for all that is worthwhile."

The Presence of God
God is with me, but more, God is within me, giving me existence. Let me dwell for a moment on God's life-giving presence in my body, my mind, my heart, and in the whole of my life.

Freedom
Lord, may I never take the gift of freedom for granted. You gave me the great blessing of freedom of spirit. Fill my spirit with your peace and your joy.

Consciousness
How am I really feeling? Lighthearted? Heavyhearted? I may be very much at peace, happy to be here. Equally, I may be frustrated, worried, or angry. I acknowledge how I really am. It is the real me that the Lord loves.

The Word
The Word of God comes down to us through the Scriptures. May the Holy Spirit enlighten my mind and my heart to respond to the gospel teachings. (Please turn to the Scripture on the following pages.

Inspiration points are provided should you need them. When you are ready, return here to continue.)

Conversation

Jesus, you speak to me through the words of the gospels. May I respond to your call today. Teach me to recognize your hand at work in my daily living.

Conclusion

I thank God for these few moments we have spent alone together and for any insights I may have been given concerning the text.

Sunday 27th March
Easter Sunday of the
Resurrection of the Lord

Luke 24:13–35

Now on that same day two of them were going to a village called Emmaus, about seven miles from Jerusalem, and talking with each other about all these things that had happened. While they were talking and discussing, Jesus himself came near and went with them, but their eyes were kept from recognizing him. And he said to them, "What are you discussing with each other while you walk along?" They stood still, looking sad. Then one of them, whose name was Cleopas, answered him, "Are you the only stranger in Jerusalem who does not know the things that have taken place there in these days?" He asked them, "What things?" They replied, "The things about Jesus of Nazareth, who was a prophet mighty in deed and word before God and all the people, and how our chief priests and leaders handed him over to be condemned to death and crucified him. But we had hoped that he was the one to redeem Israel. Yes, and besides all this, it is now the third day since these things took place. Moreover, some women of our group astounded us. They were at the tomb early this morning, and when they did not find his body there, they came back and told us that they had indeed seen a vision of angels who said that he was alive. Some of those who were with us went to the tomb and found it just as the women had said; but they did not see him." Then he said to them, "Oh, how foolish you are, and how slow of heart to believe all that the prophets have declared! Was it not necessary that the Messiah should suffer these things and then enter into his glory?" Then beginning with Moses and all the prophets, he interpreted to them the things about himself in all the Scriptures. As they came near the village to which they were going, he walked ahead as if he were going on. But they urged him strongly, saying, "Stay with us, because it is almost evening and the day is now nearly over." So he went in to stay with them. When he was at the table with them, he took bread, blessed and broke it, and gave it to them. Then their eyes were opened, and they recognized him; and he vanished from their sight. They said to each other, "Were not our hearts burning within us while he was talking to us on the road, while he was opening the Scriptures to us?" That same hour they got up and returned to Jerusalem; and they found the eleven and their companions gathered together. They were saying, "The Lord has risen indeed, and he has appeared to Simon!" Then they told what had happened on the road, and how he had been made known to them in the breaking of the bread.

- The trudging disciples had turned their backs on Jerusalem and were picking over the story as they knew it. So it was that Jesus found them, coming near and walking with them. I let him fall in step with me now.

- Jesus, find me where I am. Draw near and walk with me. Help me to recognize how my story comes to life as I listen to yours. Let me so hear your good news that my heart may glow. Let me forget myself and receive your Spirit. You bring me the message of Life, and you trust me to do for others what you want to do for me.

Suscipe

Take, Lord, and receive all my liberty,
my memory, my understanding,
and my entire will,

all I have and call my own.
You have given all to me.

To you, Lord, I return it.
Everything is yours; do with it what you will.
Give me only your love and your grace;
that is enough for me.

—St. Ignatius of Loyola

Prayer to Know God's Will

May it please the supreme and divine Goodness
To give us all abundant grace
Ever to know his most holy will
And perfectly to fulfill it.

—St. Ignatius of Loyola